COOKING FOR COMPANY

Norma MacMillan

GOLDEN PRESS / NEW YORK
Western Publishing Company, Inc.
Racine, Wisconsin

CONTENTS

This edition published 1984 by Golden Press
Library of Congress Catalog Card Number: 84-80341
ISBN 0-307-09962-8
Golden® and Golden Press® are registered trademarks
of Western Publishing Company, Inc.

First published in the U.K. by Cathay Books,
59 Grosvenor Street, London W1

This edition prepared
under the supervision
of Joanna Morris

INTRODUCTION

Company's coming – whether it's family or friends, 4 or 24, formal or casual, it's up to you to make the occasion memorable. And the best place to start is with good food.

On the pages that follow you will find new and inspiring cooking ideas. The recipes, collected from all over the world, give you the choice of exotic, sophisticated or just plain simple and delicious. Many of the dishes can be prepared in advance to let you escape the kitchen and enjoy the party as much as your guests.

Remember that the most successful parties are those that have been carefully planned – with special attention to the occasion, the food and drink and the guest list. A good mixture of guests is essential to the success of any entertaining venture. So, think ahead, use your imagination, relax and savor your triumph.

NOTES:

Always preheat the oven to the specified temperature.

Margarine can be substituted for butter in all recipes.

If substituting dried herbs for fresh, use a third of the amount; if substituting fresh for dried, use 3 times the amount.

COCKTAIL FOODS

Chicken-Stuffed Ham Rolls

3 to 3½ cups minced
  cooked chicken
⅔ cup mayonnaise
½ cup chopped
  parsley
½ cup chopped
  celery leaves
12 pitted black
  olives, finely
  chopped
1 large green pepper,
  seeded and
  chopped
Salt and pepper
16 slices cooked
  ham

Combine the chicken, mayonnaise, parsley, celery leaves, olives and green pepper and season with salt and pepper. Lay the ham slices flat and spread them with the chicken mixture; roll up. Arrange the ham rolls on a serving platter.

16 servings

Smooth Salmon Mousse

1¼ cups milk
3 peppercorns
1 bay leaf
¼ teaspoon ground mace
1 onion, stuck with 2 cloves
1 small carrot, quartered
1 envelope gelatin, softened in 2 tablespoons water
⅔ cup dry white wine
3 tablespoons butter
2 tablespoons flour
¼ cucumber, sliced
2 eggs, separated
2 cans (3½ oz each) salmon, drained
Salt and pepper
2 to 3 tablespoons half-and-half

In a small saucepan, combine the milk, peppercorns, bay leaf, mace, onion and carrot and allow to simmer over very low heat for 15 minutes.

In a separate saucepan, combine the softened gelatin and the wine. Place in warm water until the gelatin is dissolved. Pour a small amount into a 1-quart mold and let set. Keep remaining gelatin mixture warm.

Strain the milk into a saucepan. Add the butter and flour, and bring to a boil, whisking constantly. Remove from heat and let cool slightly.

Meanwhile, arrange cucumber slices in the mold. Cover with a small amount of the warm gelatin and allow to set. Keep remaining gelatin warm.

Beat the egg yolks, one at a time, into the milk mixture. Add the salmon and season with salt and pepper. Puree the mixture in a blender until smooth.

Stir in the remaining gelatin and the half-and-half. Beat the egg whites until stiff; fold into the salmon mixture. Turn into the mold and chill 2 hours, until set.

Unmold; garnish with pickle and cucumber slices and lemon twists.

6 servings

Nutty Cheese Log

1 cup cottage cheese
½ cup crumbled
   blue cheese
6 pitted black olives,
   chopped
2 tablespoons
   chopped pimiento
2 tablespoons finely
   chopped green
   pepper
1 tablespoon
   chopped parsley
3 tablespoons
   softened butter
½ teaspoon paprika
1 cup finely chopped
   walnuts

Combine the cottage cheese and blue cheese in a mixing bowl. Stir in the olives, pimiento, green pepper, parsley, butter and paprika; mix well.

Shape the mixture into a log about 2 inches in diameter. Wrap in waxed paper and chill until firm.

Unwrap and roll the log in chopped walnuts until well coated. Wrap in fresh waxed paper and chill until ready to serve. To serve, cut into slices.

Makes 20 slices

Hot Crabmeat Canapés

2 tablespoons butter
½ small onion,
   finely chopped
½ small green
   pepper, seeded and
   finely chopped
1 can (6½ oz)
   crabmeat, flaked
1 cup grated Cheddar
   cheese
4 tablespoons catsup
2 teaspoons
   Worcestershire
   sauce
Pinch of cayenne
   pepper

Melt the butter in a medium saucepan. Add the onion and green pepper and sauté over a low heat until softened. Stir in the crabmeat, cheese, catsup, Worcestershire and cayenne and simmer gently, stirring, over a low heat until the cheese is melted and the mixture is hot. Spread on melba toast or small toast rounds or squares and serve hot.

Makes about 40 canapés

Tarragon Egg Squares

2 slices bacon
4 hard-cooked eggs,
  finely chopped
2 tablespoons heavy
  cream
1 teaspoon tarragon
  vinegar
1 teaspoon dried
  tarragon
Cocktail bread or
  melba toast
2 to 3 tablespoons
  mayonnaise

Cook the bacon until crisp; drain and crumble. Combine the bacon, eggs, cream, vinegar and tarragon in a mixing bowl; chill until firm.

Spread the mixture on the cocktail bread. Spread a thin layer of mayonnaise on top and arrange on a baking sheet.

Broil for about 1 minute, or until lightly browned. Serve hot.
Makes about 40 canapés

9

Cheesy Olive Roll-Ups

30 large pimiento-stuffed green olives
2 cups grated Cheddar cheese
10 slices bacon

Cut the olives in half lengthwise and remove the pimientos. Finely chop the pimientos; mix thoroughly with the grated cheese. Stuff the olive halves with the cheese mixture.

Cut each slice of bacon into thirds. Press two stuffed olive halves together and wrap in the bacon, securing with a wooden pick.

Arrange the olives on a baking sheet and broil for 8 to 10 minutes, turning once or twice, or until the bacon is completely crisp.

Makes 30 roll-ups

Seeded Crackers

24 water biscuits or other plain crackers
4 tablespoons butter, melted
Caraway, poppy or sesame seeds

Brush one side of each cracker with the melted butter. Sprinkle with caraway, poppy or sesame seeds and arrange the crackers in one layer on a baking sheet. Bake in a 350° oven for 5 minutes, or until crisp and hot.

Makes 24 crackers

Soy Toasted Almonds

1 lb blanched almonds
4 tablespoons butter
2 tablespoons soy sauce
2 tablespoons dry sherry
½ teaspoon ground ginger
Garlic salt

Spread the almonds on a rimmed baking sheet and toast in a 300° oven for 20 minutes.

Meanwhile, melt the butter in a small saucepan. Stir in the soy sauce, sherry and ginger. Pour over the almonds and continue to toast for 15 to 20 minutes, turning the almonds once or twice.

Season the almonds with garlic salt. Spread on paper towels to dry and cool.

12 to 16 servings

Caraway Cheese Spread

1 cup cottage cheese
1 cup butter,
   softened
½ teaspoon paprika
½ teaspoon caraway
   seeds
½ small onion,
   grated

In a medium mixing bowl, cream together the cottage cheese and butter. Add the paprika, caraway and onion and mix well. Season with additional paprika and caraway seeds if desired. Serve with crackers.

10 to 12 servings

11

Apple and Date Dip

1 package (8 oz)
   cream cheese,
   softened
2 red apples, grated
12 pitted dates,
   finely chopped
Milk

Combine the cream cheese, apples and dates in a medium mixing bowl and mix thoroughly, adding just enough milk to achieve a dipping consistency. Cover and chill for at least 2 hours before serving. Serve in a bowl surrounded by apple slices and topped with chopped dates.

6 to 8 servings

Tangy Tuna Dip

1 can (7 oz) tuna,
   drained
1 package (3 oz)
   cream cheese
2 tablespoons
   mayonnaise
1 tablespoon
   chopped capers
½ teaspoon soy
   sauce
1 teaspoon prepared
   horseradish
¼ teaspoon garlic
   salt
¼ teaspoon celery
   salt
Milk

In a large mixing bowl combine the tuna, cream cheese, mayonnaise, capers, soy sauce, horseradish, garlic salt and celery salt; mix well. If the mixture is too thick for dipping, add a small amount of milk to give it a dipping consistency. Serve on a bed of endive spears and garnish with capers.

6 to 8 servings

Dill Cheese Dip

½ cup cottage
   cheese
1 package (3 oz)
   cream cheese
½ onion, grated
6 stuffed green
   olives, chopped
½ teaspoon dried dill
Salt
Half-and-half

Combine the cheeses, onion, olives and dill in a mixing bowl. Season with salt and mix thoroughly. Add enough half-and-half to give the mixture a dipping consistency. Serve garnished with dill or chives.

6 servings

Guacamole with Crudités

2 ripe avocados
Juice of ½ lemon
2 tomatoes, peeled,
   seeded and
   chopped
½ onion, grated
1 clove garlic,
   minced
½ teaspoon
   Worcestershire
   sauce
¼ cup yogurt
Salt and pepper
½ small cauliflower
4 carrots
4 stalks celery
½ cucumber
1 green pepper
1 red pepper

Halve the avocados and remove the pits. Scoop the flesh into a bowl and mash with the lemon juice. Add the tomatoes, onion, garlic, Worcestershire, yogurt and salt and pepper to taste. Beat thoroughly until smooth and turn into a serving dish.

Break the cauliflower into flowerets and cut the remaining vegetables into matchstick pieces.

Place the dip on a large plate and surround with the vegetables.

Makes about 2 cups dip

Hummus

1 can (16 oz) chick
   peas
2 tablespoons tahini
2 cloves garlic,
   chopped
Juice of ½ lemon
2 tablespoons olive
   oil
½ teaspoon salt
¼ teaspoon pepper

Place the chick peas and their juice in
an electric blender. Add the remaining
ingredients and puree until smooth
and creamy. Check the seasonings.

Arrange on a bed of lettuce and garnish with chopped mint. Serve with an
assortment of crackers.

Makes about 2 cups dip

APPETIZERS

Cold Vegetable Platter

1 large head
   cauliflower
1 lb green beans
1 can (16 oz) sliced
   beets
2 green peppers
2 red peppers
4 hard-cooked eggs,
   sliced
1¼ cups Vinaigrette
   (page 72)

Cut the cauliflower into flowerets and cook for 2 to 3 minutes in boiling water. Drain and refresh under cold water. Pat dry and arrange on a section of a large platter.

Trim the beans. Cook in boiling water and refresh under cold water. Arrange on the platter.

Drain the beets well and pat the slices dry with paper towels. Arrange on the platter.

Seed the peppers and cut them into rings. Arrange by color on the platter. Chill

Mound the egg slices in the center. Pour Vinaigrette over the salad and let guests serve themselves.

12 servings

Mushrooms à la Grecque

2 tablespoons olive
oil
1 medium onion,
finely chopped
1 clove garlic,
minced
1 lb mushrooms,
stemmed
2/3 cup dry white
wine
2 tablespoons
tomato puree
1 teaspoon sugar
Bouquet garni
Salt and pepper

Heat the oil in a large skillet over moderate heat. Add the onion and garlic and sauté until softened. Add the mushrooms, wine, puree, sugar, bouquet garni and season with salt and pepper. Let simmer, uncovered, over a moderately low heat for 20 minutes. Remove from the heat and let cool.

Transfer to a serving dish, removing the bouquet garni. Chill until serving time. Garnish with chopped parsley and serve with crisp, warm rolls.

6 servings

Pears with Blue Cheese

4 ripe pears
4 teaspoons lemon
  juice
½ lb blue cheese
1⅓ cups yogurt
Salt and pepper

Leaving the stems on, peel the pears. Carefully remove the core with an apple corer. Brush each pear with lemon juice to prevent discoloration. Crumble and cream the cheese with a fork until soft. Stuff each pear with about 2 tablespoons of the cheese. Combine the remaining cheese with the yogurt and blend well. Season with salt and pepper to taste.

Place the pears on individual salad plates, lined with lettuce if desired. Carefully coat each pear with dressing. Garnish with mint leaves.

4 servings

Smoked Whitefish Mousse

⅔ lb boned smoked
  whitefish
1 cup milk
1 bay leaf
2 tablespoons butter
2 tablespoons flour
2 tablespoons lemon
  juice
½ cup heavy cream
Salt and pepper

Combine the whitefish, milk and bay leaf in a saucepan and bring to a boil over high heat. Reduce heat to low, cover and simmer for 10 minutes. Strain, reserving the milk. Flake the fish.

Melt the butter in a small saucepan and blend in the flour. Gradually add the reserved milk, stirring, and bring to a boil. Reduce heat and simmer, stirring until thickened.

Remove from heat and stir in the lemon juice and the flaked fish. Whip the cream until thickened and fold into the mixture. Season with salt and pepper to taste.

Transfer to individual ramekins and chill before serving. Garnish with cucumber slices.

4 servings

Stuffed Mushrooms

24 large mushrooms
½ cup butter
1 clove garlic,
minced
1 cup bread crumbs
½ cup grated
Parmesan cheese
2 tablespoons
chopped parsley
Salt and pepper

Remove the caps from the mushrooms and set aside. Chop the stems finely. Melt half of the butter in a large skillet. Add the mushroom stems and garlic and sauté until softened. Stir in the bread crumbs, cheese and parsley and season to taste. Remove from the heat.

Melt the remaining ¼ cup butter and pour about half of it into a shallow baking dish. Arrange the mushroom caps, rounded tops down, in the baking dish. Spoon a heaping portion of the bread crumb mixture into each mushroom cap. Sprinkle with the remaining butter.

Bake in a 350° oven for about 15 minutes, or until the filling is lightly browned.

6 servings

Dressed Hearts of Celery

2 bunches celery
½ cup mayonnaise
   or salad dressing
¼ cup sour cream
¼ cup catsup
¼ cup tomato
   chutney
1½ teaspoons
   Worcestershire
   sauce
1 teaspoon prepared
   horseradish
Few drops hot
   pepper sauce
Salt
2 hard-cooked eggs,
   sliced
2 green onions,
   finely chopped

Cut the root ends and tops from the celery bunches, trimming to about 6 inches and cutting each lengthwise in half. Cook in boiling salted water for 4 to 6 minutes, or until just tender. Place in a colander under running cold water; drain and chill.

Meanwhile, in a small mixing bowl combine the mayonnaise, sour cream, catsup, chutney, Worcestershire, horseradish and hot pepper sauce and season with salt. Chill.

Top the celery with the egg slices, dressing and green onions. Serve remaining dressing on the side.

6 servings

Fanned Eggs and Salami

1 cup cottage cheese
¼ lb Brie, rind
   removed
24 thin slices salami
8 hard-cooked eggs
24 small thin slices
   cucumber
24 small thin slices
   tomato
24 large thin slices
   radish
2 tablespoons
   French dressing
2 teaspoons chopped
   parsley

Beat the cottage cheese with the Brie until very soft and smooth. Spoon into a pastry bag fitted with a large star tip.

Arrange 3 slices of salami on each of 8 serving plates. Pipe a ring of the cheese mixture on each bed of salami, making a "nest" about 2 inches in diameter for each egg.

Lay each egg on its side and make several cuts about halfway through each egg. Gently fan out the egg, using a sharp knife to insert slices of cucumber, tomato and radish between the cuts.

Perch each egg in the center of the cheese "nests" on serving plates. Sprinkle with French dressing and parsley. Garnish with watercress.
8 servings

Egg and Anchovy Pâté

2 cans (2 oz each)
   anchovy fillets
8 stuffed green
   olives, halved
2 tablespoons butter
1 medium onion,
   chopped
1 to 2 cloves garlic,
   minced
4 tablespoons flour
⅔ cup milk
⅔ cup chicken broth
3 eggs, beaten
1 cup bread crumbs
¼ cup capers
3 hard-cooked eggs,
   chopped
Pepper

Grease a 1-quart loaf pan and line the bottom with waxed paper. Arrange 8 anchovies and the olives in the pan. Chop the remaining anchovies and reserve, with their oil.

Melt the butter in a skillet and add the onion and garlic; sauté over low heat for 5 minutes. Stir in the flour. Add the milk and broth a little at a time, stirring. Bring to a boil and boil, stirring. until thickened. Remove from the heat and add the reserved anchovies and oil. Cool slightly and add beaten eggs, bread crumbs, capers and hard-cooked eggs. Season with pepper. Let stand for 15 minutes; then spoon into the pan.

Bake in a 350° oven for 1 hour, or until set. Let stand until cold. Turn onto a platter.

8 to 10 servings

Rabbit Pâté

⅔ cup bread crumbs
⅔ cup milk
1 lb boned rabbit,
    coarsely chopped
½ lb boned pork loin,
    coarsely chopped
1 egg, beaten
¼ teaspoon ground
    nutmeg
1 teaspoon Dijon
    mustard
Salt and pepper
3 bay leaves
8 slices bacon

Combine the bread crumbs and milk in a small bowl and soak for 10 minutes. Strain, pressing out the excess milk.

In a mixing bowl, combine the bread crumbs, rabbit, pork, egg, nutmeg and mustard. Add salt and pepper.

Place the bay leaves in the bottom of a 1-quart loaf pan. Line the bottom and sides of the pan with bacon, stretching the slices to fit if necessary. Spoon the meat mixture into the pan, pressing down firmly. Cover with buttered foil.

Place in a large roasting pan containing water about half the depth of the loaf pan. Bake in a 350° oven for 2 hours, or until the juices run clear.

Remove the pâté from the water and weight the top with a heavy object; let cool. Chill overnight.

Turn the pâté out onto a serving platter, slice and garnish with parsley. Serve with Mustard Bread or Herbed Bread (see opposite page).

6 to 8 servings

Mustard Bread

1 cup butter,
  softened
1 to 2 tablespoons
  Dijon or French
  mustard
1 loaf French bread,
  cut in half
  lengthwise

Cream the butter with the mustard until well blended.

Spread a thick layer of the mustard mixture on each loaf half. Wrap each in foil and bake in a 400° oven for 20 minutes.

Serve hot, thickly sliced.

6 to 8 servings

Herbed Bread

1 loaf French bread
½ cup butter,
  softened
1 clove garlic,
  minced
2 teaspoons lemon
  juice
1½ teaspoons
  oregano

Slice the loaf, cutting almost all the way through to the bottom crust.

Cream the butter with the garlic, lemon juice and oregano until well blended.

Spread the butter between the slices of bread, wrap in foil and bake in a 300° oven for 8 to 10 minutes, until hot. Serve at once.

6 to 8 servings

Pâté Maison

1 lb ground veal
1½ lb ground pork
2 cloves garlic, halved
2 large onions, sliced
¾ cup dry white wine
2 tablespoons brandy
2 tablespoons oil
Salt and pepper
½ lb sliced bacon

Combine the veal and pork in a glass bowl and mix well. Sprinkle the garlic and onions on top and pour the wine, brandy and oil over all. Cover and refrigerate overnight.

Remove and discard onion. Mince the garlic halves and blend into the meat with the liquid. Season with salt and pepper.

Line a 9 × 5 × 3-inch loaf pan with some of the bacon. Spoon in the meat mixture, smoothing the top. Cover with the remaining bacon and then with foil.

Place in a roasting pan containing about 1 inch of hot water. Bake in a 375° oven for 2 hours or until the pâté has shrunk away slightly from the sides of the pan and there is no trace of pink in the juices. Weight the top of the pâté and let cool. Refrigerate overnight; turn out to serve.

8 to 10 servings

Shrimp in Wine

1 lb medium shrimp, shelled and cooked
6 tablespoons dry white wine
1 cup rice
2 tablespoons butter
1 clove garlic, minced
2 tablespoons dry sherry
Salt
¼ cup grated Parmesan cheese

Place the shrimp in a glass bowl and sprinkle with the wine. Let marinate for 2 hours, turning occasionally.

Meanwhile, cook the rice according to package directions; keep warm.

Melt the butter in a large skillet. Add the garlic and sauté until softened. Stir in the shrimp, wine and sherry and season with salt. Simmer over low heat only until the shrimp are heated through. Stir in the cheese; remove from heat.

Divide the rice among warmed serving plates and top with the shrimp; garnish with chopped parsley.

4 servings

Creamy Liverwurst Spread

5 oz liverwurst
1 package (8 oz)
    cream cheese,
    softened
2 cloves garlic,
    minced
1 tablespoon
    chopped parsley
2 to 3 tablespoons
    milk

Combine the ingredients in a mixer bowl and beat until soft. Add milk if consistency is too hard. Transfer to a serving bowl and serve with toast points.

6 servings

Variations:
• Sauté 2 tablespoons chopped mushrooms in 1 tablespoon oil until softened. Drain and stir into the spread before serving.
• Sauté 1 finely chopped onion in 1 tablespoon oil until soft. Drain and combine with the other ingredients.

Ceviche

1 lb sole fillets,
    coarsely diced
Juice of 2 lemons
4 tomatoes, diced
1 green pepper,
    seeded and diced
4 tablespoons olive
    oil
1 tablespoon white
    wine vinegar
2 tablespoons
    chopped parsley
Salt and pepper

Combine the fish and lemon juice in a glass bowl and let marinate for at least 3 hours or, preferably, overnight in the refrigerator.

Add the tomatoes, green pepper, olive oil, vinegar and parsley and season with salt and pepper; mix thoroughly. Chill.

To serve, mound the ceviche on 6 lettuce-lined plates. Garnish with thin avocado and black olive slices.

6 servings

Herbed Cheese Soufflé

3 tablespoons butter
6 tablespoons flour
1¼ cups
 half-and-half
3 eggs, separated
5 oz Boursin cheese,
 crumbled
Salt and pepper

Melt the butter in a medium saucepan. Add the flour and cook, stirring, for 1 minute. Remove from the heat and stir in the half-and-half little by little, mixing well between each addition. Return to a moderate heat and bring to a boil, stirring; simmer until thickened.

Remove from the heat and let cool slightly. Beat in the egg yolks, one at a time. Add the cheese and stir until melted. Season with salt and pepper and let cool.

Beat the egg whites until stiff peaks form. Mix a small amount into the cheese mixture, then fold in the remaining egg whites.

Turn the mixture into a buttered 1-quart soufflé dish. Place on a baking sheet and bake in a 375° oven for 35 to 40 minutes, until well risen and golden brown. Serve immediately.

3 to 4 servings

Tomato and Cheese Soufflé

2 tablespoons butter
1 clove garlic,
 minced
1 small onion,
 chopped
1 can (16 oz) whole
 tomatoes, drained
 and chopped
2 teaspoons dried
 oregano
8 pitted black olives,
 chopped
Salt and pepper
Herbed Cheese
 Soufflé (see above)

Melt the butter in a large skillet. Add the garlic, onion and tomatoes and sauté over a moderately low heat for 3 to 4 minutes. Stir in the oregano and olives, and season with salt and pepper. Allow to cool.

Meanwhile, prepare the soufflé.

Spread the tomato mixture in the bottom of a buttered 1½-quart soufflé dish. Pour in the soufflé mixture. Place the soufflé dish on a baking sheet and bake in a 375° oven for 35 to 40 minutes, until well risen and golden brown. Serve immediately.

4 servings

ENTRÉES

Filet Mignon with Roquefort

3 oz Roquefort
  cheese
3 tablespoons butter,
  softened
1 tablespoon port
1 teaspoon each
  chopped chives
  and thyme
½ clove garlic,
  minced
Salt and pepper
6 beef tenderloin
  steaks (1 inch
  thick)

Place the cheese, butter and port in a blender and puree. Stir in the herbs, garlic and salt and pepper. Form the mixture into a log about 1½ inches in diameter; wrap in foil and chill in the freezer for 20 minutes.

Sprinkle a layer of salt into a large preheated skillet and sauté the steaks for 3 to 5 minutes on each side, depending on desired doneness.

Slice the butter in 6 thick pats. Serve the steaks topped with the butter.
6 servings

Beef Birds with Tomatoes

12 slices (2 oz each)
  beef sirloin,
  pounded
12 thin slices
  mortadella
2 tablespoons oil
1 clove garlic, thinly
  sliced
1 teaspoon dried
  thyme
1 teaspoon dried
  basil
2/3 cup dry white
  wine
1 can (16 oz) whole
  tomatoes
1 can (2¼ oz) tomato
  puree
Salt and pepper

Lay the sirloin slices on a flat surface. Top each with a slice of mortadella, roll up jelly-roll fashion and secure with a wood pick.

Heat the oil in a large skillet, add the meat and brown on all sides. Remove from the skillet and drain.

Pour the excess fat from the skillet. Stir in the garlic, thyme, basil, wine and tomatoes with their juice. Bring to a boil and boil rapidly for 10 minutes. Stir in the tomato puree. Season with salt and pepper.

Return the meat rolls to the pan, cover and simmer over a low heat for 35 to 40 minutes. Just before serving, remove the cover and increase the heat to let the sauce reduce and thicken slightly.

6 servings

Cheese Ring with Cold Cuts

⅓ cup vinaigrette
   dressing
⅓ cup mayonnaise
1½ lb cottage cheese
Salt and pepper
¾ lb potatoes,
   cooked and diced
4 hard-cooked eggs,
   chopped
1 green pepper,
   seeded and diced
1 jar (2 oz) chopped
   pimiento, drained
1 onion, minced
3 tablespoons
   chopped parsley
Sliced cooked
   tongue, ham or
roast beef

In a large mixing bowl, combine the vinaigrette and mayonnaise. Add the cottage cheese and season with salt and pepper. Fold in the potatoes, eggs, green pepper, pimientos, onion and parsley. Spoon the mixture into a lightly greased 6-cup ring mold. Chill for at least 2 hours.

Roll up the tongue, ham or beef slices. Carefully unmold the cheese ring onto a platter. Arrange the rolled meat around the cheese ring and fill the center with radishes and black olives.

8 servings

NOTE: This recipe can be doubled for a large buffet party.

Jellied Beef

1 beef brisket (5 lb), thin end
2 onions
6 whole cloves
1 celery stalk with leaves
2 cloves garlic
1 bay leaf
6 black peppercorns
1 tablespoon Worcestershire sauce
2 envelopes unflavored gelatin, softened in ¼ cup water

In a large saucepan, combine the beef, onions, cloves, celery, garlic, bay leaf, peppercorns and Worcestershire. Add enough water to cover and bring to a boil. Skim the surface of any residue. Reduce the heat and simmer, partially covered, for 3½ hours, or until the beef is tender.

Remove the beef from the pot. Boil the cooking liquid rapidly until it is reduced to about 4 cups. Season to taste with salt. Skim off any fat and strain. Stir in the softened gelatin until dissolved.

Slice the beef across the grain and cut into short strips. Press into a loaf pan or bowl large enough to hold the meat. Pour the reduced stock over the beef. Cover with foil or a plate. Weight with heavy cans and chill overnight.

To serve, unmold and garnish as desired.

10 to 12 servings

Chili Con Carne

3 tablespoons oil

3 onions, finely chopped

2 medium green peppers, seeded and diced

2 red chilies, seeded and diced (optional)

2 cloves garlic, minced

3 lb lean ground beef

3 cans (16 oz each) whole tomatoes, chopped

4 tablespoons tomato paste

2 teaspoons chili powder

2 bay leaves

3 cans (16 oz each) red kidney beans, drained

Salt and pepper

Heat the oil in a large saucepan. Add the onions, green peppers, chilies and garlic and sauté until softened. Add the beef and continue cooking, stirring to break up the meat, until browned. Stir in the tomatoes and their juice, tomato paste, chili powder and bay leaves. Cover and simmer over a low heat for 1 hour.

Stir in the kidney beans and season to taste with salt and pepper. Simmer, uncovered, for 30 minutes. Discard the bay leaves before serving.

10 to 12 servings

NOTE: for a hotter flavor, add more chili powder.

Swedish Meatballs

3 lb lean ground beef
1 cup grated
  Parmesan cheese
2 onions, finely
  chopped
1 clove garlic,
  minced
3 eggs, beaten
1 teaspoon grated
  nutmeg
Salt and pepper
3 tablespoons butter
2½ cups beef broth
2 teaspoons tomato
  paste
2 egg yolks, beaten
2 cups sour cream
4 tablespoons dried
  dill

Combine the beef, cheese, onions, garlic, eggs and nutmeg in a mixing bowl. Season with salt and pepper and mix well. Form into walnut-size balls.

Melt half the butter in a large skillet. Add the meatballs, browning a few at a time and transferring to a casserole. Use more butter as needed until all meatballs are well browned.

Combine the broth and tomato paste in the top of a double boiler. Add the egg yolks and cook, stirring, over simmering water for 5 minutes. Take care not to let mixture become too hot or egg yolks will scramble. Remove from the heat and stir in the sour cream and dill. Pour the sauce over meatballs and cook in a 300° oven for 20 minutes.

Serve hot in a chafing dish.

10 to 12 servings

African Curried Lamb

2 tablespoons butter
2 tablespoons oil
2½ lb boneless
  stewing lamb, cut
  into 1-inch cubes
2 onions, chopped
2 cloves garlic,
  crushed
2 tablespoons curry
  powder
¼ to ½ teaspoon
  chili powder
4 tablespoons cider
  vinegar
2 bay leaves
1 can (16 oz) whole
  tomatoes,
  chopped
¼ cup currant jelly

Melt the butter in the oil in a large saucepan. Sear the meat in 3 batches, removing it when browned.

Add the onions and garlic to the pan and sauté until softened. Blend together the curry powder, chili powder and vinegar and stir into the onions. Cook for 1 minute.

Return the lamb cubes to the pan and stir in the bay leaves, tomatoes and their juice and jelly. Mix well, cover and simmer over low heat for 2 hours, or until the lamb is tender.

Uncover, increase heat and boil rapidly until the liquid has reduced and thickened slightly. Remove and discard bay leaves. Serve with small bowls of chopped green pepper, tomato wedges, banana slices and chutney.

6 servings

Coriander Lamb Chops

2 cloves garlic,
  thinly sliced
½ teaspoon chili
  powder
2 teaspoons ground
  ginger
1 teaspoon ground
  coriander
2 tablespoons
  chopped coriander
  leaves
⅔ cup yogurt
Salt and pepper
4 lamb chops

Combine the garlic, chili powder, ginger, ground coriander, coriander leaves and yogurt in a mixing bowl.

Arrange the chops in a shallow dish; spoon the yogurt mixture over them and cover. Marinate for 2 hours.

Remove the chops from the marinade and place on a broiler pan. Broil under moderately high heat, basting occasionally with marinade, for 8 to 10 minutes on each side, until cooked through and browned.

4 servings

Roast Lamb and Herb Sauce

1 leg of lamb (6 to 7 lb)
2 small onions
4 whole cloves
2 cloves garlic
2 carrots, sliced
12 peppercorns
12 juniper berries (optional)
4 parsley sprigs
2 bay leaves
2 mint sprigs
2 thyme sprigs
1½ cups dry white wine
3 tablespoons oil
Salt and pepper
2 tablespoons butter
3 shallots or green onions, finely chopped
4 tablespoons flour
1 can (10½ oz) beef broth
4 tablespoons chopped parsley

Place the lamb in a large sturdy plastic bag. Add the onions, cloves, garlic, carrots, peppercorns, juniper berries, herbs and wine. Close the bag securely and refrigerate for 2 days, turning the bag occasionally.

Remove the lamb, reserving the marinade, and place on a rack in a roasting pan. Rub lamb with the oil and season with salt and pepper. Roast in a 450° oven for 15 minutes. Reduce the heat to 350° and continue roasting for 1½ hours or until lamb is cooked to desired doneness.

Meanwhile, strain the marinade into a saucepan. Bring to a boil and boil until reduced to 1¼ cups.

In another saucepan, melt the butter. Add the shallots and sauté until softened. Add the flour and cook, stirring, for 2 minutes. Gradually stir in the reduced marinade and broth. Bring to a boil, stirring, and simmer until thickened. Add the parsley. Pass the sauce on the side.

6 to 8 servings

Broiled Leg of Lamb

2 cloves garlic, crushed
¾ cup dry red wine
5 tablespoons olive oil
5 tablespoons red wine vinegar
¼ cup chopped parsley
1 teaspoon mixed dried herbs
Salt and pepper
1 leg of lamb (6 to 7 lb), boned and butterflied

In a roasting pan, combine the garlic, wine, oil, vinegar, parsley and herbs and season with salt and pepper. Place the lamb in the pan and marinate for 1 hour, turning from time to time.

Lay the lamb in a preheated broiler, fat side up, about 5 inches below the heat. Broil, basting occasionally with the marinade, for 20 minutes on each side, or until the lamb is cooked through.

6 to 8 servings

Pork Tenderloin and Pâté

2 pork tenderloins
1 can (4 oz) smooth
    pâté
Salt and pepper
2 tablespoons butter
1 clove garlic,
    minced
¼ cup chopped
    mushrooms
⅔ cup dry sherry
⅔ cup dry white
    wine
1 teaspoon Dijon
    mustard
Dash of
    Worcestershire
    sauce
½ teaspoon mixed
    herbs
2 tablespoons heavy
    cream
2 tablespoons
    chopped chives
1 tablespoon capers
    (optional)

Using a sharp knife, make a long, straight lengthwise cut through the center of each tenderloin, cutting about three-quarters through. Spread the pâté amply over the cut surfaces; press back together and tie or sew up securely. Season with salt and pepper.

Melt the butter in a large skillet. Add the meat and brown. Remove from the pan and drain on paper towels.

Add the garlic to the pan and sauté briefly. Add the mushrooms and sauté 1 minute. Add the sherry, wine, mustard, Worcestershire and herbs; bring to a boil. Return the pork to the pan, reduce heat, cover and simmer 35 to 40 minutes, turning occasionally.

Remove pork from the pan and keep warm. Increase the heat and boil the cooking liquid until thickened. Add cream and boil for 2 minutes. Add the chives and capers.

Slice the pork and arrange on a warmed platter. Spoon the sauce over and serve immediately.

4 to 6 servings

42

Marinated Sicilian Pork Kabobs

If sage leaves are unavailable, add a good pinch of dried ground sage to the marinade.

4 tablespoons olive oil
2 tablespoons lemon juice
1 clove garlic, crushed
1 tablespoon mixed herbs
Salt and pepper
1½ lb pork tenderloin, cut into 1-inch cubes
4 slices French bread (1 inch thick), quartered
8 slices Black Forest ham, halved and rolled up
Sage and bay leaves

Combine the oil, lemon juice, garlic and herbs in a shallow dish, season with salt and pepper and mix well. Add the pork cubes and let marinate for 1 to 2 hours, turning occasionally. Remove the meat from the dish, reserving the marinade.

Thread the pork, French bread and ham rolls alternately on 8 skewers, interspersing with sage and bay leaves.

Broil under moderately high heat or over a charcoal grill, basting with the reserved marinade, for 10 minutes on each side, until the pork is tender and browned.

Serve hot, with vegetables and a green salad.

4 to 6 servings

Pork Chops with Barbecue Sauce

This wonderfully spicy barbecue sauce not only adds zest to the chops, it makes them tender and succulent as well.

2 tablespoons oil
1 onion, chopped
2 cloves garlic, minced
2 tablespoons tomato puree
2 tablespoons red wine vinegar
3 tablespoons Worcestershire sauce
3 tablespoons honey
½ teaspoon chili powder
½ teaspoon dry mustard
Salt
1 can (8 oz) whole tomatoes
6 pork chops
Salt and pepper

Heat the oil in a small saucepan. Add the onion and garlic and sauté until softened. Add the tomato puree, vinegar, Worcestershire, honey, chili powder, dry mustard, salt and tomatoes. Bring to a boil, reduce the heat and simmer for 15 minutes.

Season the chops well with salt and pepper. Place in a large shallow oven-proof dish and bake in a 375° oven for 15 minutes.

Drain any excess fat from the chops and turn them. Cover with the sauce and return them to the oven for 15 minutes, or until tender.

6 servings

Lemon-Pear Pork Chops

5 tablespoons oil
6 center cut pork
    loin chops
1 onion, chopped
¾ cup orange juice
Salt and pepper
3 firm pears, peeled,
    halved and cored
2 tablespoons brown
    sugar
6 thin slices lemon
Whole cloves
2 teaspoons
    cornstarch

Heat the oil in a large skillet. Add the chops and brown on both sides. Arrange in one layer in a shallow oven-proof dish.

Add the onion to the skillet and sauté until softened. Spoon onto the chops and pour the orange juice over. Season with salt and pepper. Cover and bake in a 375° oven for 20 minutes.

Fill the cavity of each pear half with 2 teaspoons brown sugar and top each with a lemon slice secured with cloves. Place a pear on each chop and bake, uncovered, for 10 minutes.

Transfer the chops and pears to a warmed platter and keep hot. Skim the fat from the cooking liquid and strain into a measuring cup. Add water to bring to ¾ cup and pour into a sauce-pan. Dissolve the cornstarch in a little water and add to the pan. Cook, stirring, until thickened. Pour over the chops and serve.

6 servings

Veal Scallops with Tomatoes

2 tablespoons oil
2 cloves garlic,
 thinly sliced
1 lb thinly sliced veal
 scallops, pounded
 flat
Salt and pepper
1 cup dry white wine
1 can (16 oz) whole
 tomatoes, drained
 and chopped
Dash of
 Worcestershire
 sauce
1 tablespoon tomato
 puree
1 teaspoon each
 dried oregano and
 marjoram

Heat the oil in a skillet. Add the garlic
and sauté for 1 minute. Season the veal
with salt and pepper; add to the skillet
and brown quickly on both sides.

Drain off any oil. Add the wine and
the tomatoes to the veal, bring to a boil
and boil rapidly for 10 minutes. Stir in
the Worcestershire, tomato puree and
herbs and simmer for 5 minutes.

Transfer to a warmed serving platter
and serve immediately, garnished
with dill sprigs.
4 servings

Veal Birds with Mushrooms

12 small veal
   scallops, pounded
   flat
6 slices cooked ham,
   cut into halves
12 green onions,
   trimmed
¼ lb sharp Cheddar
   cheese, cut into 12
   sticks
3 tablespoons butter
3 tablespoons oil
½ lb mushrooms,
   sliced
¾ cup dry white
   wine
1 teaspoon soy sauce
Salt and pepper

Lay the veal scallops on a flat surface. Place a half ham slice, a green onion and a stick of cheese on each scallop and roll up. Tie with string or secure with wood pick.

Melt the butter in the oil in a large skillet. Add the veal rolls and brown; remove from the skillet as they brown.

Add the mushrooms to the skillet and sauté for 5 minutes. Stir in the wine and soy sauce, season to taste with salt and pepper and bring to a boil. Return the veal rolls to the pan and simmer, covered, over moderate heat for 10 minutes, or until meat is tender.
6 servings

47

Orange Baked Chicken

2 eggs, beaten
6 tablespoons orange
  juice
1 cup bread crumbs
1½ teaspoons grated
  orange rind
1 teaspoon paprika
Salt and pepper
2 chickens (2½ to
  3 lb each),
  quartered
½ cup butter, melted

Beat the eggs with the orange juice in a shallow dish. Combine the bread crumbs, orange rind and paprika on a sheet of waxed paper and season the mixture with salt and pepper. Dip the chicken in the egg mixture, then coat with the seasoned crumbs.

Pour half the melted butter into a large ovenproof dish. Arrange the chicken, skin side down, in one layer in the dish and drizzle with the remaining butter. Bake in a 350° oven for 1 hour, turning halfway through the cooking.

Serve garnished with orange wedges and watercress.

6 servings

Tarragon Chicken

½ lb butter
3 tablespoons
 chopped tarragon
Salt and pepper
1 chicken (5½ to 6 lb)
2 tablespoons flour
¾ cup heavy cream

Cream the butter with the chopped tarragon and season with salt and pepper. Carefully loosen the skin of the breast. Tuck one quarter of the tarragon butter under the skin on each side of the breast. Form the remaining butter into a ball and place in the cavity.

Place the chicken in a roasting pan and roast in a 375° oven for 1½ hours, basting occasionally with pan juices, until the leg moves easily when pushed. Transfer to a warmed serving platter.

Skim the excess fat from the pan juices. Blend the flour with the cream and stir into the pan juices. Simmer over moderate heat, stirring, until thickened.

Serve the sauce separately.

4 to 6 servings

Chicken Cacciatore

2 chickens (2½ to 3 lb each), cut into pieces
Salt and pepper
4 tablespoons butter
3 tablespoons olive oil
1 onion, chopped
2 cloves garlic, crushed
½ lb mushrooms, sliced
¾ to 1 cup dry white wine
¼ cup chicken broth
1 can (16 oz) whole tomatoes, drained and chopped
4 tablespoons tomato paste
2 bay leaves
1 teaspoon dried basil

Rub the chicken pieces with salt and pepper. Melt the butter in the oil in a Dutch oven. Add the chicken pieces, in batches, and brown on all sides; remove from the pot as they brown.

Add the onion and garlic to the pot and sauté until softened. Add the mushrooms and sauté for 2 minutes. Stir in the wine, broth, tomatoes, tomato paste, bay leaves and basil and bring to a boil.

Return the chicken pieces to the pot, reduce the heat and simmer, uncovered, for 10 minutes. Cover and continue simmering for 20 minutes. Remove and discard the bay leaves, adjust the seasonings and serve.

6 to 8 servings

Honey Curry Chicken

⅓ cup butter
½ cup honey
1½ teaspoons curry powder
6 tablespoons prepared mustard
Salt and pepper
8 skinned chicken breast halves

Melt the butter in a small saucepan. Stir in the honey, curry powder and mustard; season with salt and pepper. Cook, stirring, until well blended.

Arrange the chicken in one layer in an ovenproof baking dish. Cover with the honey mixture, turning the chicken to coat well all over.

Bake in a 350° oven for 1 hour, turning over midway through cooking.

8 servings

Chicken Livers in Marsala

1 lb chicken livers
2 tablespoons butter
2 onions, chopped
1 clove garlic,
    crushed
½ teaspoon chili
    powder
¼ lb mushrooms,
    sliced
⅔ cup Marsala
1 teaspoon dried
    mixed herbs
Dash of
    Worcestershire
    sauce
Salt and pepper
⅔ cup cream

Trim the chicken livers and rinse thoroughly in water; pat dry on paper towels.

Melt the butter in a large skillet. Add the onions and garlic and sauté until lightly browned. Stir in the chili powder and chicken livers and sauté for 5 minutes. Stir in the mushrooms and Marsala; simmer for 5 minutes. Add the herbs and Worcestershire; season with salt and pepper. Add the cream, increase the heat, bring to a boil and boil for 2 minutes, stirring, until the sauce is thickened.

Serve over hot cooked rice. Garnish with thyme sprigs, if available.

4 to 6 servings

Chicken with Walnuts

4 green onions
½ cup walnuts
2 whole boned and
    skinned chicken
    breasts
1 sweet red pepper
2 zucchini
2 tablespoons oil
2 cloves garlic, sliced
1 small piece
    gingerroot,
    chopped
2 oz button
    mushrooms
2 oz Chinese pea
    pods
2 tablespoons soy
    sauce
1 tablespoon dry
    sherry

Roughly chop the green onions and walnuts. Thinly slice the chicken, red pepper and zucchini.

Heat the oil in a large skillet or wok over high heat. Add the garlic, ginger and onions and stir-fry for 1 minute. Add the chicken and cook, stirring, for 2 minutes. Add the remaining ingredients and cook, stirring constantly, for 3 minutes.

Serve immediately.

4 servings

Chicken Breasts in Vermouth

1 tablespoon oil
1 clove garlic, thinly
　sliced
1 large onion, sliced
6 boned and skinned
　chicken breast
　halves
Salt and pepper
⅔ cup dry white
　vermouth
1 tablespoon
　chopped parsley
1 teaspoon dried
　tarragon
⅔ cup cream

Heat the oil in a large skillet. Add the garlic and onion and sauté until lightly browned. Remove to a plate and set aside.

Season the chicken with salt and pepper. Add to the skillet and brown. Return the onion and garlic to the skillet, increase the heat and add the vermouth and herbs. Boil over high heat for 12 to 15 minutes, turning the chicken twice. Transfer the chicken to a warmed platter and keep hot.

Add the cream to the skillet and boil over high heat, stirring, until the sauce has thickened.

Spoon the sauce over the chicken and garnish with lemon slices and tarragon sprigs, if available.

6 servings

53

Crispy Duck with Grapes

1 duckling (3 to 4 lb),
  split
1 teaspoon salt
1 teaspoon
  arrowroot
⅔ cup orange juice
¼ lb seedless red
  grapes, halved

Rub the duckling halves with salt. Place on a rack in a roasting pan and bake in a 450° oven for 30 minutes. Reduce heat to 350° and bake 1 hour, or until juices run clear when pierced with a fork.

Meanwhile, blend the arrowroot with the orange juice in a small saucepan. Bring to a boil. Stir in the grapes. Pour the sauce over the duckling.

2 servings

Cassoulet

1 lb dried Great
  Northern beans,
  soaked overnight
½ lb lean bacon,
  chopped
4 cloves garlic,
  chopped
2 tablespoons oil
1 lb boned shoulder
  of lamb, cubed
2 or 3 chicken
  thighs, halved
Bouquet garni
2 cups chicken broth
Pepper
¼ lb piece of
  Kielbasa sausage
1 can (14 oz) whole
  tomatoes
1 tablespoon tomato
  puree
1 teaspoon sugar
Salt and pepper
½ cup dry bread
  crumbs

Drain the beans, cover with fresh water and place in a saucepan. Bring to a boil, add the bacon and garlic and simmer for 1½ hours. Drain.

Heat the oil in a separate skillet and sauté the lamb and chicken until evenly browned. Add to the beans, along with the bouquet garni, broth and plenty of black pepper. Cover and simmer for 2 hours. Add the sausage and simmer for 1 hour, or until the beans are tender, adding more chicken broth if necessary.

Meanwhile, place the tomatoes and their juice, puree, sugar and salt and pepper in a skillet. Bring to a boil, stirring; then simmer for 20 minutes, until thickened. Cool.

Transfer the beans to a large ovenproof dish. When cool, slice the sausage and return it to the dish. Spoon the tomato pulp over the top and sprinkle with bread crumbs. Bake in a 375° oven for 30 minutes.

4 to 6 servings

Shrimp in Sherry Herb Sauce

4 tablespoons butter
¼ cup olive oil
3 cloves garlic,
    minced
2 tablespoons
    minced parsley
8 basil leaves,
    shredded
½ cup dry sherry
1½ lb shrimp,
    shelled and
    deveined

Melt the butter with the oil in a large skillet. Add the garlic and sauté for 3 minutes. Add the parsley and basil and sauté lightly for 3 minutes. Pour in the sherry and simmer for 5 minutes. Remove from heat.

Place the shrimp in a shallow baking dish and cover with the sauce. Broil until opaque and pink, 3 to 5 minutes.

Divide the shrimp among the plates and serve over hot rice, spooning the sauce over the shrimp.

4 servings

Quick Paella

1 lb shrimp
2 or 3 lean thick
  slices bacon
¼ lb chorizo or pork
  sausage links
2 tablespoons oil
3 cloves garlic, sliced
1 cup rice
4 tomatoes, chopped
⅔ cup dry white
  wine
⅔ cup chicken broth
Salt and pepper
1 sweet red pepper,
  chopped
Few strands saffron
1 can (14 oz)
  artichoke hearts
12 mussels

Peel and devein the shrimp and set aside. Dice the bacon and slice the sausage.

Heat the oil in a large skillet, add the garlic and sauté until softened but not brown. Add the bacon and sauté for 5 minutes. Stir in the rice, tomatoes, wine and broth and season with salt and pepper. Bring to a boil; reduce heat and simmer for 5 minutes. Add the red pepper, sausage and saffron. Simmer for 10 to 12 minutes.

Drain, rinse and quarter the artichoke hearts. Add to the pan with the mussels and shrimp and cook for 5 minutes.

4 to 6 servings

Creole-Style Shrimp

1 onion
1 clove garlic
2 celery stalks
1 green pepper
1 tablespoon oil
1 can (16 oz) whole
    tomatoes, drained
Salt and pepper
4 tablespoons dry
    white wine
1 tablespoon tomato
    puree
1½ lb shrimp, peeled
2 drops hot pepper
    sauce
1 teaspoon
    Worcestershire
    sauce
1 tablespoon
    chopped parsley

Chop the onion and garlic. Slice the celery and finely chop the pepper.

Heat the oil in a large skillet. Add the onion and garlic and sauté until lightly browned. Add the celery and sauté for 2 minutes. Add the pepper and tomatoes to the skillet and season with salt and pepper. Stir in the wine and tomato puree, breaking up the tomatoes. Bring to a boil; reduce heat and simmer, uncovered, for 20 minutes.

Stir in the shrimp, pepper sauce and Worcestershire. Simmer for 5 minutes; then stir in the parsley. Serve immediately.

4 to 6 servings

Mediterranean Seafood

1 tablespoon butter
2 shallots, chopped
⅔ cup dry white
    wine
2 tablespoons dry
    sherry
1 teaspoon Dijon
    mustard
Pinch of cayenne
    pepper
Dash of
    Worcestershire
    sauce
⅔ cup light cream
2 cans (6½ oz each)
    crabmeat, drained
1 lb shrimp, cooked
    and peeled
Salt and pepper
Grated Parmesan
    cheese

Melt the butter in a large skillet, add the shallots and sauté until softened, but not brown. Add the wine and sherry, bring to a boil and boil rapidly until reduced by half.

Stir in the mustard, cayenne and Worcestershire and boil for 2 minutes. Add the cream, return to a boil and boil for 5 minutes, stirring occasionally, or until thickened.

Remove from the heat, stir in the crabmeat and shrimp and season with salt and pepper. Heat through and serve, sprinkled with the cheese.

4 servings

Tarragon Chicken Mousse

3 eggs, separated
2 tablespoons
    cornstarch
²⁄₃ cup chicken broth
1 envelope gelatin,
    softened in 2
    tablespoons water
²⁄₃ cup sour cream
1 tablespoon
    tarragon vinegar
2 teaspoons dried
    tarragon
1½ cups minced
    cooked chicken
Salt and pepper

Blend the egg yolks with the cornstarch and broth in a saucepan. Simmer over moderate heat, stirring constantly, until thickened; do not boil.

Remove from the heat and add the gelatin, stirring to dissolve. Stir in the sour cream, vinegar, tarragon and chicken. Season well with salt and pepper. Refrigerate until the mixture is just beginning to set, stirring occasionally. Beat the egg whites until just stiff; fold in gently but thoroughly.

Turn into a 1½-quart mold and refrigerate for about 4 hours, or until set.

Unmold onto a serving platter and garnish with lemon slices and tarragon or watercress.

4 to 6 servings

Blue Cheese Mousse

1 can (10½ oz) beef
consommé
Cucumber slices
4 tablespoons butter
2 onions, chopped
2 cloves garlic,
minced
4 tablespoons
cornstarch
1½ cups milk
1 bay leaf
¾ lb blue cheese,
crumbled
2 egg yolks
2 to 3 tablespoons
half-and-half
1 tablespoon
chopped parsley
Salt and pepper

Pour a small amount of the consommé
into the base of a 1½-quart mold;
arrange a few cucumber slices in the
consommé and refrigerate to set.

Melt the butter in a saucepan. Add
the onions and garlic and sauté until
softened. Remove from the heat and
stir in the cornstarch. Gradually stir in
the milk. Add the bay leaf and cheese
and bring to a boil, stirring.

Cool slightly. Discard bay leaf and
beat in egg yolks, one at a time. Sieve or
puree in a blender until smooth.

Stir in the half-and-half, remaining
consommé and parsley and season
with salt and pepper. Pour into the
mold and chill overnight. Unmold and
garnish with cucumber and rosemary
or parsley.

6 to 8 servings

61

VEGETABLES & SALADS

Asparagus with Hollandaise

2 lb asparagus
HOLLANDAISE:
3 egg yolks
2 tablespoons fresh
  lemon juice
¼ teaspoon salt
¼ teaspoon pepper
½ cup butter, melted

Peel the tough ends of the asparagus if necessary. Place the spears in a skillet of boiling water. Cover the pan and cook over high heat for 5 minutes, or until tender.

Meanwhile, make the Hollandaise: Combine the egg yolks, lemon juice and salt and pepper in a blender. Mix until just combined. Slowly add the butter until the sauce is thick.

Divide the asparagus among dinner plates and top with Hollandaise. Pass the remaining sauce on the side.

4 to 6 servings

Broccoli with Maltaise Sauce

2 bunches broccoli
MALTAISE SAUCE:
3 egg yolks
2 tablespoons fresh
  lemon juice
¼ teaspoon salt
¼ teaspoon pepper
½ cup butter, melted
3 tablespoons fresh
  orange juice
1½ teaspoons grated
  orange rind

Trim the broccoli and divide into flowerets. Arrange in a steamer over water. Cover tightly and steam until still somewhat firm but tender, 10 to 12 minutes.

Meanwhile, make the Maltaise Sauce: Combine the egg yolks, lemon juice, salt and pepper in a blender. Mix until just combined. Slowly add the butter and blend until the sauce is thick. Add the orange juice and orange rind and blend until thick.

Serve the broccoli topped with the sauce.

6 to 8 servings

French Fried Zucchini

1 lb zucchini
½ cup flour
Salt and pepper
Oil for deep-frying

Cut the zucchini in quarters lengthwise; then cut into "fingers," each about 2 inches long. Put the flour in a large paper or plastic bag, season with salt and pepper, add the zucchini and shake to coat well.

Heat the oil in a deep fryer to 375°. Fry the zucchini, in batches, until well browned. Drain on paper towels. Plunge into the hot oil briefly just before serving. Drain and season.

6 servings

Duchesse Potatoes

1½ lb baking
  potatoes, boiled
⅓ cup butter
1 egg, beaten
Salt and pepper

Mash the potatoes while still hot, and immediately beat in the butter and egg; season with salt and pepper. Spoon into a pastry bag fitted with a large star tip. Pipe into decorative swirls on a baking sheet. Bake in a 400° oven for 20 minutes, until crisp and golden.

6 servings

French-Style Peas

4 lettuce leaves
3 green onions
2 packages (10 oz each) frozen peas
⅔ cup water
1 teaspoon lemon juice
1 teaspoon sugar

Shred the lettuce and slice the green onions. Combine all ingredients in a saucepan. Bring to a boil. Reduce heat, cover and simmer for 5 minutes; drain.

Transfer to a warmed serving dish, dot with butter and serve.
6 servings

Ratatouille

3 tablespoons olive oil
2 onions, sliced
2 cloves garlic, chopped
1 eggplant, sliced
1 green pepper, seeded and sliced
½ lb zucchini, sliced
2 tomatoes, sliced
Salt and pepper

Heat the oil in a 3-quart flameproof casserole. Add the onion and garlic and sauté gently until softened. Add the eggplant and sauté 5 minutes, turning frequently. Add the pepper, zucchini and tomatoes and season with salt and pepper. Stir well. Cover and bake in a 350° oven for 1 hour. Serve hot.
6 servings

NOTE: Ratatouille can also be served cold as a first course.

Tri-Color Vegetable Puree

1 lb parsnips, cut
  into pieces
1 lb carrots, cut into
  pieces
1 lb Brussels sprouts
⅔ cup heavy cream
6 tablespoons butter
Salt and pepper

Cook the parsnips, carrots and sprouts separately in boiling salted water.

In a blender puree each vegetable separately, adding ⅓ each of the cream and the butter. Place in stainless steel bowls and season with salt and pepper. Just before serving, cover with a damp towel and heat through, about 5 minutes in a 350° oven.

To serve, arrange the purees in stripes on an oblong dish or in neat mounds on a round dish.

6 servings

NOTE: Celeriac, kohlrabi and turnips can be prepared in the same way.

Brussels Sprouts and Chestnuts

2 lb Brussels sprouts
  or 3 packages
  (10 oz each) frozen
  Brussels sprouts
¾ cup butter
1 jar (8 oz) roasted
  peeled chestnuts,
  halved
Salt and pepper

Trim the fresh sprouts and steam them for 10 minutes, or until tender. (If using frozen sprouts, cook according to package directions and drain.)

Melt the butter in a skillet. Add the sprouts and chestnuts and sauté, tossing, until thoroughly coated with the butter and heated through. Season with salt and pepper and serve hot.

6 to 8 servings

Glazed Baby Carrots

2 lb baby carrots,
  scraped and
  trimmed
4 tablespoons butter
2 tablespoons sugar

Boil the carrots, covered, in lightly salted water to just cover for 8 minutes. Add the butter and sugar and cook, uncovered, for 4 to 5 minutes more, until the water evaporates. Toss the carrots until well coated with the caramelized sugar and butter sauce.

6 to 8 servings

Party Baked Potatoes

Baked potatoes with fancy fillings are inexpensive but elegant companions that turn plain meats into party fare.

4 large baking
   potatoes
Oil for brushing
Butter

Brush the potatoes all over with the oil, place on a baking sheet and bake in a 400° oven about 1 hour, until soft.

Remove from the oven, immediately cut a large deep cross in the top of each and fill generously with butter. Serve plain or with one of the following fillings.

4 servings

BACON AND ONION FILLING:

4 tablespoons butter
1 large onion, finely
   chopped
Salt and pepper
8 slices lean bacon,
   cooked crisp and
   crumbled
1 tablespoon
   chopped parsley
4 tablespoons grated
   Parmesan cheese

Remove the potatoes from the oven and cut in half lengthwise. Scoop out the flesh and mash until smooth.

Melt the butter in a skillet, add the onion and sauté until golden brown. Stir the onion into the potatoes and season with salt and pepper. Add the bacon and parsley and mix well. Spoon the mixture back into the skins and sprinkle with the cheese. Bake for 15 to 20 minutes.

4 servings

SOUFFLÉ CHEESE FILLING:

2 eggs, separated
1 cup grated sharp
   Cheddar cheese
1 teaspoon prepared
   hot mustard
Salt and pepper

Remove the potatoes from the oven and cut in half lengthwise. Scoop out the flesh and mash until smooth. Beat in the egg yolks, cheese and mustard and season with salt and pepper.

Beat the egg whites until stiff. Fold into the mixture. Spoon back into the potato skins, sprinkle with grated Parmesan cheese if desired and bake for 15 to 20 minutes.

4 servings

CHIVE AND SOUR CREAM FILLING:

2 egg yolks
²/₃ cup sour cream
Dash of hot pepper sauce
2 tablespoons chopped chives
Salt and pepper

Remove the baked potatoes from the oven and cut in half lengthwise. Scoop out the flesh and mash until smooth. Beat in the egg yolks, sour cream, hot pepper sauce and chives and season with salt and pepper. Spoon the mixture back into the skins and place on a baking sheet. Bake for 15 to 20 minutes, until hot and golden brown.
4 servings

Herbed-Stuffed Tomatoes

6 medium tomatoes
1 bunch green
   onions, thinly
   sliced
2 cups bread crumbs
3 slices bacon,
   cooked and
   crumbled
2 tablespoons each
   chopped parsley
   and basil
2 tablespoons bacon
   fat or olive oil
1 clove garlic,
   minced

Remove the stems from the tomatoes and cut off the tops. Spoon out the pulp and chop; combine it in a bowl with the remaining ingredients. Add salt and pepper if necessary.

Divide the stuffing among the tomatoes and place them in a baking dish.

Bake in a preheated 350° oven for 15 to 20 minutes, until heated through. Serve hot.

6 servings

Tomato Aspic with Mayonnaise

1 can (3.5 oz) tomato
    puree
2 tablespoons lemon
    juice
1 tablespoon sugar
1 bay leaf
1 teaspoon each
    dried tarragon and
    basil
Salt and pepper
2 envelopes
    unflavored gelatin
½ cup tomato juice
1 cup sliced celery
½ cup chopped green
    pepper
12 each pitted black
    and stuffed green
    olives
MAYONNAISE:
2 egg yolks
2 teaspoons Dijon
    mustard
1½ tablespoons
    lemon juice
Salt and pepper
1 cup olive oil

Combine the tomato puree, lemon juice, sugar, bay leaf, tarragon and basil in a saucepan. Cook over moderately high heat until hot. Pass through a strainer and season to taste with salt and pepper.

Dissolve the gelatin in the tomato juice. Stir it into the hot juice and mix. Add water to make 5 cups. Pour the liquid into a 6- to 7-cup ring mold and chill until slightly firm.

Combine the celery, pepper and olives and add them to the partially set aspic. Chill until firm.

Place all of the mayonnaise ingredients except the oil in a blender and whirl to just combine. Add ¼ cup of the oil and whirl. Slowly add the remaining oil and blend until smooth and thick.

Unmold the aspic and serve with a bowl of mayonnaise in the center.

8 to 12 servings

Cherry Tomato Sauté

2 pints cherry
    tomatoes
3 tablespoons butter
1 tablespoon olive
    oil
2 tablespoons
    chopped parsley

Remove the stems from the tomatoes and prick each one with a pin.

Melt the butter with the oil in a skillet. Add the tomatoes and sauté, tossing, for 3 to 4 minutes, until heated through. Sprinkle with the parsley and serve hot.

6 to 8 servings

Wild Rice Salad

1½ cups wild rice,
  cooked
1¼ cups Vinaigrette
  (see below)
3 tablespoons
  Oriental sesame
  oil
2 stalks celery, sliced
1 green pepper,
  seeded and cut
  into rings
1 red pepper, seeded
  and cut into rings
¼ pound snow pea
  pods, trimmed
½ pint cherry
  tomatoes, halved
2 tablespoons
  minced fresh
  coriander or
  parsley
12 pitted black
  olives, halved
Salt and pepper

Combine the ingredients in a large bowl and toss to mix thoroughly. Serve chilled or at room temperature.
6 to 8 servings

Vinaigrette for Green Salad

Greens
1 cup olive oil
¼ cup wine vinegar
2 tablespoons lemon
  juice
1 clove garlic,
  minced
1 teaspoon dry
  mustard
1 teaspoon salt
1 teaspoon pepper

Allow 2½ to 3 oz trimmed salad greens and 2 tablespoons dressing for each portion. For 25, this translates into about 4¾ lb of untrimmed greens and 3 cups dressing. Tear or cut the greens into bite-size pieces and garnish if desired. Use any of the following:
GREENS: Belgian endive, Bibb, Boston, curly endive, iceberg, watercress.
GARNISHES: Sliced cucumbers, mushrooms, radishes, onions, tomatoes or zucchini; artichoke hearts, bean sprouts, croutons.

To make the dressing combine the ingredients in a jar and cover tightly. Shake to blend. Pour over greens just before serving.
Makes about 1¼ cups

Cucumber Salad

4 medium
   cucumbers
1 large onion, cut
   into rings
1 cup sour cream
2 tablespoons oil
1 tablespoon cider
   vinegar
1 teaspoon sugar
Salt and pepper

Peel the cucumbers and halve them lengthwise. Remove the seeds and slice thin.

In a bowl, combine the cucumbers and onion. Add the remaining ingredients and toss until combined. Chill before serving.

6 to 8 servings

Lentil Salad

2½ cups lentils,
  cooked, drained
  and chilled
1 cup Vinaigrette
  (page 72)
4 green onions,
  thinly sliced
3 tablespoons
  chopped parsley
3 tomatoes, diced
2 zucchini, diced
Salt and pepper

In a bowl, combine the lentils with the Vinaigrette and toss well. Add the green onions, parsley, tomatoes and zucchini and toss to coat. Season to taste with salt and pepper. Chill or serve at room temperature, garnished with chopped parsley.
6 to 8 servings

Noodles in Sesame Sauce

¼ cup sesame paste
2 tablespoons
  boiling water
1 lb noodles,
  whole-wheat
  spaghetti or
  linguine, cooked
3 green onions,
  thinly sliced

Combine the sesame paste with the boiling water. Stir to make a smooth paste. Toss with the warm pasta until coated. Combine with the green onions and serve warm or chilled.
4 to 6 servings

NOTE: If sesame paste is unavailable, substitute ¼ cup peanut butter combined with 2 tablespoons Oriental sesame oil and omit the boiling water.

Pasta Salad

1 lb corkscrew or
  shell-shaped pasta
1 cup Vinaigrette
  (page 72)
¼ lb snow pea pods,
  trimmed
1 sweet red pepper,
  seeded and diced
½ lb mushrooms,
  sliced
3 stalks celery,
  thinly sliced
1 bunch green
  onions, sliced

Cook the pasta according to package directions. Drain and cool in cold water; drain well. Toss with the Vinaigrette. Add the remaining ingredients and toss gently to mix. Serve at room temperature.
6 to 8 servings

DESSERTS

Biscuit Tortoni

2 cups heavy cream
½ cup granulated
    sugar
5 egg yolks
⅓ cup powdered
    sugar
1 tablespoon dark
    rum
1½ cups macaroon
    crumbs

Whip the cream, slowly adding the granulated sugar. Refrigerate.

Beat the egg yolks until light. Slowly beat in the powdered sugar and rum. Continue beating until the mixture falls from the beaters in a ribbon.

Gently fold ¼ cup of the macaroon crumbs into the egg yolk mixture. Fold in the whipped cream until just blended.

Spoon the mixture into small cups or stemmed wine glasses and freeze until firm.

Just before serving, sprinkle the tops of the tortoni with the remaining macaroon crumbs.
8 to 10 servings

Coffee Crème Caramel

⅓ cup granulated
   sugar
1 tablespoon water
3 eggs
2 tablespoons
   superfine sugar
2 cups milk
1 tablespoon instant
   coffee

In a small heavy-bottom skillet, combine the granulated sugar and water and warm over low heat until the sugar has dissolved. Increase the heat and boil rapidly until golden brown. Pour immediately into 8 buttered 1-cup ramekins or a 1-quart mold. Let cool.

Beat the eggs and superfine sugar in a mixing bowl. Warm the milk over a low heat, stir in the instant coffee and beat the milk into the eggs.

Strain the mixture into the ramekins. Place in a roasting pan with enough hot water to come halfway up the dishes. Bake in a 325° oven for 40 to 45 minutes for individual sizes, about 1 hour for the large one, or until set.

Let cool. Invert on a platter and serve.

8 servings

Key Lime Pie

¼ cup brown sugar

2 cups zwieback crumbs

4 tablespoons butter, melted

1 envelope gelatin, softened in 2 tablespoons water

Grated rind and juice of 3 limes

2 eggs, separated

1 can (14 oz) condensed milk

1 cup heavy cream

Combine the sugar and zwieback crumbs in a mixing bowl. Pour in the melted butter and mix well. Turn into an 8-inch springform pan and press firmly over the bottom and side. Chill.

Place the container of softened gelatin in hot water until the gelatin is dissolved. Add to the lime juice in a large bowl, then beat in the grated rind and egg yolks. Gradually beat in the condensed milk. Let stand until just beginning to set; stir occasionally.

Beat the egg whites until stiff. Fold them into the lime mixture and turn into the crumb crust. Chill for several hours.

Whip the cream and put in a pastry bag fitted with a star tip. Pipe onto the pie. Garnish with lime slices.

6 servings

Vanilla Rice Cream

¼ cup long-grain rice

2 cups milk

¼ cup sugar

2 eggs, separated

1 teaspoon vanilla

⅔ cup heavy cream, whipped

Combine the rice, milk and sugar in a heavy-bottom saucepan and bring to a boil, stirring constantly. Reduce heat to low, cover and simmer for 40 to 45 minutes, stirring occasionally, until all the milk is absorbed and rice is soft. Remove from the heat.

Beat in the egg yolks, one at a time. Return saucepan to the heat to simmer for 1 minute, stirring constantly; do not boil. Stir in the vanilla. Sieve or work in a blender until smooth. Allow to cool.

Whisk the egg whites until stiff. Fold together with the rice mixture and cream. Spoon into long-stemmed glasses or ramekins and chill.

Garnish with chopped nuts.

6 servings

Coffee and Walnut Mousse

1 tablespoon instant coffee
2 tablespoons boiling water
4 egg yolks
¼ cup packed brown sugar
½ cup walnuts, finely ground
⅔ cup heavy cream, whipped
4 teaspoons Tia Maria (optional)

Combine the instant coffee and the boiling water in the top half of a double boiler. Stir in the egg yolks, sugar and walnuts and whisk over simmering water until creamy and thick enough to form a ribbon.

Remove the pan from the water and continue whisking until the mixture is cold and thick enough to hold its shape. Fold in the cream.

Spoon into individual serving dishes and top each with a teaspoon of Tia Maria. Garnish with a walnut half. Serve chilled.

4 servings

Plum Pudding Mousse

1 can (14 oz) purple plums
1 envelope gelatin, softened in 2 tablespoons water
1 can (6 oz) evaporated milk
3 teaspoons lemon juice
2 egg whites
¼ cup superfine sugar

Drain the juice from the plums and add enough warm water to make 1 cup. Add the softened gelatin and heat gently to dissolve. Remove the pits from the plums and puree in a blender. Stir into the juice. Chill until the mixture starts to thicken.

Meanwhile, combine the evaporated milk and lemon juice in a bowl and beat until thick and creamy. Stir in the thickened fruit mixture and let stand until just beginning to set.

Beat the egg whites until stiff, then gradually whisk in the sugar to make a soft meringue. Carefully fold the meringue into the fruit mixture.

Turn into individual dishes and chill until set. Serve garnished with whipped cream and nuts.

6 servings

Peppermint Mousse

1¼ cups heavy
  cream
½ teaspoon
  peppermint
  flavoring
2 egg whites
1 tablespoon
  superfine sugar
¼ cup chopped
  peppermint sticks

Whip the cream with the peppermint flavoring. Beat the egg whites and sugar until stiff enough to stand in peaks. Fold the beaten egg whites and chopped peppermint sticks into the whipped cream.

Spoon the mixture into individual serving dishes and place in the freezer for about 2 hours, until well chilled and just on the point of freezing. Serve immediately.

4 to 6 servings

Cold Chocolate Soufflé

1½ tablespoons
 cocoa
3 tablespoons
 boiling water
6 eggs, separated
¾ cup superfine
 sugar
2¼ teaspoons
 ground cinnamon
1½ envelopes
 gelatin, softened
 in 3 tablespoons
 water
1 cup heavy cream,
 lightly whipped
½ lb semi-sweet
 chocolate

Blend the cocoa with the boiling water to a smooth paste; cool.

Combine the egg yolks, sugar, cinnamon, gelatin and cocoa paste in the top of a double boiler. Stir over simmering water until creamy and thick enough to form a ribbon. Remove from the heat and beat until cool.

Beat the egg whites until stiff. Carefully fold the whipped cream and beaten egg whites into the custard.

Turn into a 3-cup cold soufflé dish fitted with a stiff paper collar several inches above the rim. Chill for 2 hours. Meanwhile, shave half the chocolate into curls with a potato peeler. Finely grate the remainder.

Carefully peel off the collar and press the grated chocolate around the side. Arrange chocolate curls on top.

4 to 6 servings

Crystallized Ginger Soufflé

3 oz crystallized
  ginger, minced
2 tablespoons
  boiling water
1 envelope gelatin,
  softened in 2
  tablespoons water
4 eggs, separated
2 tablespoons
  superfine sugar
⅔ cup whipping
  cream, lightly
  whipped
¾ cup chopped nuts

Place the ginger in the top of a double
boiler with the boiling water and gelatin. Add the egg yolks and sugar and
stir over simmering water until
creamy and thick enough to form a
ribbon. Remove from the water and
beat until cool.

Beat the egg whites until stiff. Fold
the egg whites and whipped cream into
the custard. Turn into a 1-quart soufflé
dish fitted with a stiff paper collar
several inches above the rim. Chill for
2 hours, or until set.

Peel off the collar carefully and press
the nuts around the side of soufflé. If
desired, decorate with additional
whipped cream and ginger.
4 to 6 servings

Baked Chocolate Soufflé

¼ cup cocoa
3 tablespoons
    cornstarch
1¼ cup milk
4 tablespoons
    superfine sugar
4 tablespoons butter
4 eggs, separated
1 teaspoon vanilla
    extract
¼ cup powdered
    sugar, sifted

Blend the cocoa and cornstarch with a little of the milk in a saucepan. Add the remaining milk, the superfine sugar and butter and simmer, stirring, until thickened. Cool slightly; then beat in the egg yolks, one at a time, and the vanilla.

Beat the egg whites until stiff. Fold about 2 tablespoons into the chocolate mixture, then fold in the remainder. Pour into a greased 1½-quart soufflé dish and bake in a 350° oven for 35 to 40 minutes, until risen and firm on the top.

Sprinkle with the powdered sugar and serve immediately.

4 servings

Milanese Soufflé

3 eggs, separated
⅓ cup superfine
    sugar
1 envelope gelatin,
    softened in 2
    tablespoons water
Grated rind and juice
    of 2 lemons
⅔ cup heavy cream,
    lightly whipped
¾ cup chopped nuts

Combine the egg yolks, sugar, gelatin and lemon rind and juice in the top of a double boiler and stir over simmering water until thick enough to form a ribbon. Remove from heat and beat until cool.

Beat the egg whites until stiff. Fold the egg whites and whipped cream into the custard. Turn into a 1-quart soufflé dish fitted with a stiff paper collar several inches above the rim. Chill for 2 hours, or until set.

Peel off the collar carefully and press nuts around the side. Decorate with cream rosettes and lemon slices.

4 to 6 servings

Lime or Orange Soufflé: Substitute rind and juice of 3 limes or 2 oranges for the lemons.
Coffee Soufflé: Replace lemons with 2 tablespoons instant coffee dissolved in 2 tablespoons water.

Glazed Banana Cream Pie

PASTRY:
1¼ cups flour
⅓ cup butter
3 tablespoons
  superfine sugar
FILLING:
1½ tablespoons
  cornstarch
1¼ cups milk
4 tablespoons
  half-and-half
4 egg yolks
1 tablespoon
  superfine sugar
½ teaspoon vanilla
1 to 2 bananas
TOPPING:
¾ cup superfine
  sugar

Sift the flour into a bowl. Add the butter and sugar and work with a fork until the mixture resembles bread crumbs. Form into a ball and knead on a lightly floured surface until smooth.

Place in the center of an 8-inch flan dish and press out until the dough completely covers the base. Prick with a fork and cover with dried beans. Bake on the top shelf of a 300° oven for about 20 minutes. Remove beans and continue baking 20 minutes longer, until lightly browned and set.

Combine the cornstarch and milk in a saucepan and bring to a boil slowly, stirring, until thickened. Reduce the heat to lowest. Beat in the half-and-half, egg yolks and sugar and heat for 2 to 3 minutes, stirring; do not boil. Cool slightly. Add the vanilla.

Slice the bananas and arrange over the cooled pastry. Cover immediately with the custard and chill until set, preferably overnight.

Sprinkle the sugar evenly over the top. Place under a broiler until the sugar caramelizes. Chill at least 2 to 3 hours before serving. Garnish with additional banana slices.

6 to 8 servings

Baked Cinnamon Cheesecake

1 package (8 oz)
    cream cheese
1 cup cottage cheese
¼ cup brown sugar
⅔ cup sour cream
2 teaspoons ground
    cinnamon
4 eggs
Pastry (see recipe
    opposite)

Soften the cream cheese in a bowl. Beat in the cottage cheese, brown sugar, sour cream and cinnamon. Beat in the eggs, one at a time.

Prepare the pastry and place in a lined and greased 8-inch springform pan. Press the pastry out to cover the base and side completely, making sure it is pressed well against side.

Pour in the cheese mixture. Bake in a 325° oven for 1 hour, until set. Leave in the pan until completely cooled.

Transfer to a serving plate and sprinkle with additional ground cinnamon. If desired, decorate with a border of whipped cream.

8 servings

Champagne Sorbet

1½ cups granulated
   sugar
1 cup water
2½ cups champagne
3 tablespoons lemon
   juice
2 egg whites
4 tablespoons
   powdered sugar

Dissolve the granulated sugar in the water in a saucepan over low heat. Bring to a boil and boil for 5 minutes, or until thick but not beginning to brown. Cool. Stir in 1½ cups of the champagne and the lemon juice. Pour into freezer trays and freeze for about 1 hour, until mushy.

Pour the mixture into a bowl and beat well for 2 minutes. Return to the freezer trays and freeze for 30 minutes. Remove and beat again. Repeat the freezing and beating every 30 minutes for 2 hours.

Beat the egg whites until stiff. Gradually beat in the powdered sugar. Remove the frozen mixture and beat well to break down the ice crystals; then fold in the meringue. Return to the freezer and freeze until firm.

Transfer the sorbet to the refrigerator to soften 30 minutes before serving. **8 servings**

Frozen Butterscotch Mousse

⅔ cup packed brown
   sugar
2 tablespoons butter
Pinch of salt
½ cup water
4 egg yolks
1 cup heavy cream
1½ teaspoons
   vanilla

In a small saucepan combine the sugar, butter and salt and warm over low heat, stirring until the sugar is dissolved and the butter melted. Bring to a boil and boil for 1 minute. Stir in the water and boil until the mixture is very smooth and syrupy. (Be careful adding the water; it may spatter.)

Beat the egg yolks in the top of a double boiler. Gradually beat in the syrup. Place over a pan of simmering water and heat, stirring constantly, until the mixture is light and fluffy. Set aside to cool.

Whip the cream with the vanilla until thick. Fold into the cooled butterscotch mixture. Pour into a mold and freeze until firm.

Transfer the mousse to the refrigerator 30 minutes before serving. To unmold, dip the mold quickly into hot water and invert onto a serving plate. Serve with fresh fruit.

6 servings

Crème Brûlée

2 cups heavy cream
3 egg yolks
¾ cup superfine
    sugar
½ teaspoon vanilla

Heat the cream in a small saucepan over a low heat. Beat the egg yolks with 1 tablespoon of the sugar in the top half of a double boiler. Add the warm cream, stirring constantly over simmering water, until the mixture thickens slightly. Add the vanilla.

Pour into six 4-ounce ramekins and bake in a 325° oven for 8 minutes. Let cool slightly. Then refrigerate until well chilled, preferably overnight.

Sprinkle each ramekin evenly with the remaining sugar. Broil under a high heat until the sugar is caramelized. Cool; then chill for about 2 hours before serving.

6 servings

Orange Sorbet

½ cup superfine
    sugar
1⅓ cups water
4 large oranges
2 teaspoons lemon
    juice
2 egg whites, beaten
    until stiff

In a small heavy-bottom saucepan, combine the sugar and water, and warm over a low heat until the sugar is dissolved completely. Bring to a boil; then simmer for 10 minutes. Cool.

Cut the tops off the oranges. Using a sharp knife, scoop out as much flesh from inside oranges as possible. Reserve the shells. Add the flesh and lemon juice to the sugar syrup. Strain the mixture into a sturdy freezer container. Cover securely and freeze for about 2 hours, until mushy.

Fold the egg whites into the orange mixture and spoon it into the orange shells. Freeze until firm, then cover with plastic wrap.

Transfer oranges to the refrigerator 1 hour before serving to soften. Garnish with shredded orange rind.

4 servings

Easy Strawberry Ice Cream

4 egg yolks
½ jar (12-oz size)
   strawberry
   preserves
1¼ cups whipping
   cream
2 tablespoons
   brandy (optional)

Beat the egg yolks in a warmed bowl for at least 5 minutes, until they thicken and turn lemon-colored. Add the preserves and beat again.

In a separate bowl, beat the cream with the brandy until it forms soft peaks. Fold the cream into the strawberry mixture and pour into a freezer container. Cover and freeze until firm.

Serve in chilled dishes.

6 servings

91

Chocolate Rum Charlotte

18 lady fingers
  (approximately)
4 tablespoons rum
3½ oz semi-sweet
  chocolate
⅓ cup packed brown
  sugar
½ cup unsalted
  butter, softened
2 eggs, separated
⅔ cup heavy cream,
  whipped

Separate the lady fingers and dip each into the rum. Place sugar side out in the base and around the side of a 6-inch soufflé dish.

Melt the chocolate in the top of a double boiler over hot water. Cream the sugar and butter until light. Stir in the chocolate while it is still hot. Beat in the egg yolks. Beat the egg whites until stiff and fold them into the mixture. Pour into the soufflé dish and chill for 24 hours.

Trim the lady fingers to the level of the filling. Invert onto a serving platter. Decorate with the whipped cream and chocolate leaves.

6 servings

NOTE: To make chocolate leaves, brush melted chocolate over backs of leaves and let dry. Strip off the leaves.

Hazelnut Meringues

4 egg whites
1 cup sugar
½ cup finely
   chopped toasted
   hazelnuts
Vanilla or chocolate
   ice cream
SAUCE:
8 oz caramels,
   chopped
1½ cups heavy
   cream

Beat the egg whites until stiff. Add 4 teaspoons of the sugar and continue beating for 1 minute. Fold in the remaining sugar and the hazelnuts. Spoon or pipe the meringue into 12 mounds on baking sheets lined with brown paper. Sprinkle with a little extra sugar.

Bake in a 180° oven for 1½ hours, turning the baking sheets around halfway through the cooking. When the meringues are done, they will not stick to the paper. Cool.

Combine the chopped caramels and cream in a saucepan and heat gently, stirring, until melted. If the sauce is too thick, add milk.

To serve, sandwich ice cream between pairs of meringues and spoon the sauce over them.

6 servings

INDEX